Collins

T0318014

Happy Handwriting

Practice Book 5

In their habitat, lions need cover like long grass or bushes in order to hide and stalk their prey. They also need water to drink.

In their habitat, ... ed cover like long grass or bushes in order to hide and stalk their prey. They also need water to drink.

Series Editor: Dr Jane Medwell
Author: Annabel Gray

William Collins' dream of knowledge for all began with the publication of his first book in 1819. A self-educated mill worker, he not only enriched millions of lives, but also founded a flourishing publishing house. Today, staying true to this spirit, Collins books are packed with inspiration, innovation and practical expertise.

They place you at the centre of a world of possibility and give you exactly what you need to explore it.

Collins. Freedom to teach.

Published by Collins
An imprint of HarperCollins*Publishers*
The News Building, 1 London Bridge Street, London, SE1 9GF, UK

HarperCollins*Publishers*
Macken House, 39/40 Mayor Street Upper, Dublin 1, D01 C9W8, Ireland

Browse the complete Collins catalogue at
collins.co.uk

10 9 8 7 6 5 4 3

ISBN 978-0-00-848584-9

British Library Cataloguing-in-Publication Data
A catalogue record for this publication is available from the British Library.

Series Editor: Dr Jane Medwell
Author: Annabel Gray
Expert Reviewer: Dr Mellissa Prunty
Publisher: Lizzie Catford
Product manager: Sarah Thomas
Project manager: Jayne Jarvis
Development editor: Abbie Rushton
Copyeditor: Alice Harman
Proofreader: Jonathan Perris
Cover designer: Sarah-Leigh Wills at Happydesigner
Design template and icons: Sarah-Leigh Wills at Happydesigner
Illustrations: Jouve India Pvt. Ltd.
Typesetter: Jouve India Pvt. Ltd.
Production controller: Alhady Ali
Printed in India by Multivista Global Pvt. Ltd.

Copy the words quickly.

is   in   on   up   over

Copy the sentences into your book as quickly as you can.

You will need to write quickly in certain situations, such as taking notes or making a shopping list. Your writing doesn't need to be perfect but you should be able to read it back.

Copy the sentence.

A cheetah is the world's fastest land mammal.

Copy the shopping list as quickly and neatly as you can.

brown bread

tinned peaches

paper plates

semi-skimmed milk

free-range eggs

milk-chocolate chips

lemonade

Copy the letters and words.

ee   re   el

tree   referee   tell

Copy the news article into your book.

Football game postponed

The Reston Rovers were disappointed yesterday when they had to postpone their game. Unfortunately, the referee had to send players home after the ball got stuck in a nearby tree.

Have you joined to e accurately?

Copy the words.

innocent   decent

confident   opponent

Copy the news article into your book.

The Rovers had a decent lead before the mishap and were confident that they would win. Some players believe that the other team kicked the ball into the tree on purpose, but their opponents claim that they are innocent.

Copy the letters.

or   ere   are   rl

Copy the passage into your book.

"Where are you?" asked Simran's friend,

Elora. She sounded worried.

"I'm in here," replied Simran, shaking.

"What are you doing in there?" Elora asked.

Copy the words.

heard	rose	write
herd	rows	right

Use the words above to complete the passage, then copy it into your book.

"Have you _____ how many people are

out there?" Simran asked. "I can't stand in front

of all those _____ of people."

"You'll be fine," said Elora. "All your friends

will be with you." Simran took a deep breath.

"You're _____. Let's do it!"

When do you still find joining r tricky?

Copy the beginning of the letter into your book.

Dear Parents/Carers,

We are writing to tell you how proud we are of the students at Edment Primary School. They have been very observant in the local area and have been reporting problems.

Choose the suffix -ant or -ent, then copy out the new word. The first one has been done for you.

observe   _observant_

obedience   assist

hesitate   differ

Copy the rest of the letter into your book.

Yesterday, we were able to assist an elderly neighbour who had fallen in the road, and to get him the help that he needed. Our pupils were obedient and followed instructions quickly so that everyone was safe in the emergency.

Yours sincerely,

Mrs Argent, Assistant Headteacher

Copy the words.

through   although

cough   thought

Copy this fact into your book. Make sure that the capital and tall letters are the correct height.

Did you know that the 'ough' spelling makes at least seven different sounds? Try saying these out loud: enough, thought, through, plough, borough, cough, although.

Copy the words.

possible   horrible   terrible

Remove the -e and add the suffix -y, then copy out the new word. The first one has been done for you.

possible   possibly   sensible

horrible   terrible

visible   incredible

Copy the fact into your notebook. Make sure that the capital and tall letters are the correct height.

When you change an adjective ending with -ble into an adverb, you remove the e and add y. For example, legible becomes legibly.

Remember, t is slightly shorter than other ascenders.

Copy the words.

Paris

Sarah

Coventry

Shola

I

Correct the capital letters and full stops in these sentences. Then copy the sentences into your book.

when choosing a holiday destination, it's important to consider what you want to experience You may want to climb the eiffel tower in paris, visit the beach in spain or snowboard in the alps

Copy the words.

Where?

Who?

How?

Why?

Add the correct capital letters and question marks into these sentences. Then copy the sentences into your book.

before booking, ask yourself these questions:

- why do I want a holiday
- who will I travel with
- how will I travel
- where will I stay

8

Copy the words quickly.

fast   *neat*   *readable*

Time yourself as you copy the passage quickly into your book. Write in the time that it takes you to finish.

Did you know that light moves at the fastest speed known in the universe? Nothing else moves as fast as light. Nothing even comes close. In a vacuum, light travels 299,793 kilometres per second – that's seriously fast!

I can write 37 readable words in _____

_____.

Time yourself as you copy the passage quickly into your book. Write in the time that it takes you to finish.

It's difficult to comprehend how fast light actually moves. To help you understand, here is a fact: it takes light from the Sun eight minutes to travel across the 150 million kilometres between the Sun and the Earth.

I can write 38 readable words in _____

_____.

Copy the words neatly.

appreciate   grateful

generous   exciting

Copy the passage neatly into your book, using your best handwriting.

Thank you so much for the generous birthday gift. I am very grateful and I appreciate your kind thought. I plan to wear my new T-shirt next week when I go out for dinner.

Use these words to help you write a 'thank you' message. Make sure to use your best handwriting.

- thank you
- appreciate
- wonderful

- dear
- surprise
- thoughtful

Using your neatest writing shows care and consideration for your reader.

Copy the words.

order   first letter

second letter

Write the list in alphabetical order in your book.

orange, apple, strawberry, pear,

watermelon, banana

Copy the sentences into your book.

If words start with the same first letter, you need

to look at the second letters to alphabetise them.

You need to look carefully to decide on the

correct alphabetical order.

Write the list of names in alphabetical order. Use the second letter of each name to help you.

Arthur

Ali

Adam

Abbie

Annabel

Astrid

Correct and quickly copy the passage into your book. Time yourself copying it.

Monday 5th January

today was a great day why because it was my

birthday and I got the most amazing present can

you guess what it was

How well do you think you have done in your writing?

I joined e.

I added the correct capitals and punctuation.

My ascenders are the right height.

Correct and quickly copy the passage into your book. Time yourself copying it.

I went downstairs and couldn't believe my eyes

a bike was in the kitchen covered in a blanket

I knew it was a bike because of the shape I

immediately got dressed and took my new wheels

out for a spin

How well do you think you have done in your writing?

My descenders are the right length.

I can write 41 readable words in _____.

Copy the sentence.

The letter t is shorter than other tall letters.

Copy the words.

interval   interpret

interact   interrupt

Copy the words.

interview

interconnect

international

Choose the correct words from above to complete the sentences. Then copy the completed sentences underneath.

I'm feeling nervous about the job _____.

We're going on an _____ flight.

The rabbits dig tunnels that _____.

Is t the right height? It should be slightly shorter than the other tall letters.

Copy the sentence.

The letter *f* can join fully to other letters.

Copy the words.

help   helpful

helpfully

Copy the sentence.

The cheerful dog was being playful in the

beautiful sunshine.

Copy the sentence.

Be careful how you write *f*.

Copy these sentences quickly.

When I'm feeling playful, I play.

But I dread feeling dreadful.

Have you joined to *f* with a diagonal join and from *f* with a horizontal join?

Copy the words.

owe   live

we   oral

Copy the sentences.

How much do we owe you?

I think you were brave to walk that way.

Copy the sentences.

Horizontal joins can go across or up.

Fill in the table with the past tense verbs. The first one has been done for you.

love	loved
live	
survive	
walk	

Do your horizontal joins go across to small letters and up to tall letters?

Copy the sentence.

Some letters do not join to the next letter.

Copy the words.

judge   yellow

grip   pale

Copy the sentence.

You told us a great joke yesterday!

Copy the sentence.

Descenders help us to recognise letters.

Copy the words.

putty   gull   young

Copy the sentence quickly.

Pretty Polly the parrot yelled at the young gull.

Have you checked that y, j, g, p are not joined to the next letter?

Copy the sentence.

Capital letters identify people, places or things.

Copy the words.

Nuneaton   Sally

Habib   Jitesh

Correct and copy the two sentences.

sally lives in nuneaton where does habib live?

Copy the alphabet in capital letters into your book. Make sure that the letters are just below the top line.

A B C D E F G H I J K L M

N O P Q R S T U V W X Y Z

Correct and copy the sentence.

all tariq wants is a trip to cornwall.

Are your capital letters the right height? They need to be just a bit shorter than the tall letters.

Copy the sentence.

Commas between items in a list need some space.

Correct the capital letters and commas in the sentence, then copy it. Then write the same sentence in your book as a list with bullet points.

My favourite cities are: tokyo paris accra rome.

Copy the sentence.

A list often uses 'and' before the last item.

Correct the capital letters, commas and full stop in the sentence, then copy it.

Paul yusuf and anya played tennis football and rounders at the sports camp

Have you left enough space for your commas, capital letters and full stop?

✎ Copy the words.

said   exclaimed

chuckled

✎ Copy the passage neatly into your book.

"I think there is something moving in the bushes," Jasmin said, looking carefully in the direction of the sound.

"I can't see anything," said Molly.

"Let's turn on our torches," whispered George.

"OK, but be really quiet," Jasmin murmured.

✎ Copy the direct speech into the sentences, adding speech marks, then copy the whole sentence into your book.

Let's go!

I'm scared.

_____ said Mia, clapping her hands. Jake looked embarrassed and whispered, _____

Have you left enough space to place the speech marks clearly?

19

Copy the words.

I'm

she'll

they've

you'd

Correct and copy the sentences.

Im not sure if hes arrived yet.

Shes late I dont think theyre ever on time.

Copy the words.

can't

won't

couldn't

don't

Correct and copy the sentences.

I cant do it! I wont do it! said the boy,

stamping his foot. He didnt understand why

they werent listening to him.

Have you left enough space for the apostrophes?

✎ Copy the words.

order   first letter

second letter

✎ Write these words in alphabetical order in your book, using the first and second letter of each item.

potatoes, carrots, courgettes, peas,

celery, cucumber, parsnips

✎ Copy the sentence.

If the first letters of words are the same, use

their second letters to alphabetise them.

✎ Copy these words in alphabetical order, using the first and second letter of each name.

Mike

Myla

Mahmood

Mustafa

Melody

Have you checked the words' second letters?

Correct and then neatly copy the sentence into your book.

to make perfect birthday pancakes, you'll need: eggs milk flour butter salt blueberries don't forget a frying pan!

How well do you think you have done in your writing?

I joined to and from t and f.

I put commas in between items in a list.

My capitals are the right height.

Correct and then quickly copy the passage into your book. Time yourself copying it.

Method

Put the eggs milk flour and salt into a bowl and mix carefully. next, pour the mixture into a frying pan. once cooked, add the blueberries on top. Enjoy!

I can write 30 readable words in _____

_____.

Copy the words.

point   idea   topic

Read the passage, underline two key points and then write them out quickly.

Lions can live in different environments, such as open grasslands and woodlands, but there must be sufficient prey available for them to survive.

1.

2.

Copy the words quickly.

notes   bullets   details

Read the passage, underline two key points and then write them out quickly.

Lions need cover, such as long grass or bushes, in their habitat, in order to stalk their prey. They also need water to drink – although not every day – so they look for water sources in the dry season.

1.

2.

Copy the words.

lock   cricket

king   knit

Copy the sentences into your book.

If I were king, I'd play cricket all day.

If I were king, I'd knit all day.

If I were king, I'd eat cake all day.

Copy the words.

kick   trek

sock   kitten

Trace over the first letters, on the left side. Then match the first letters with the correct endings, to make four words. The first one has been done for you. Then write a sentence for each word.

l   icket
b   acket
t   ucket
j   ocket

Copy the words.

ending   sending

action   motion

Copy the passage into your book.

Yesterday, I planned an adventure for my family. We boarded the train early and headed into London. We arrived at Waterloo and rode on the London Eye.

Copy the words.

principal   principle

whether   weather

Use the words above to complete the sentences. Then copy the completed sentences.

The teacher took Sajid to see the _____.

I was hoping for sunny _____ today.

Do your joins to round letters go over and back?

Copy the words.

partial confidential

essential potential

Copy the sentences neatly.

The official notes are confidential. It is essential that they are given special attention.

Copy the words.

finance commerce

province

Copy the passage quickly into your book.

Breaking news

Some financial businesses in New York are moving to a more provincial setting, after claims that the area is becoming too commercial and overcrowded.

Are your ascenders tall and parallel to one another?

Copy the words in print.

Road

Avenue

Close

Hill

Copy the two addresses into your book. Left-align them and use printed capital letters for the postcode.

6 Lamplight Road

Spooky Hollow

Hamington

51749

Cedar Cottage

Rosemary Walk

Shady Green

HR6 4JH

Copy the sentence in print.

Writing that is not joined is called printing.

These addresses haven't been written neatly. Can you write them correctly in your book?

Flat 15

4 Hare Way

Little Hopping

r-3478

Skiffle Building

Liverpool

lv23 8WS

Have you left-aligned the addresses and printed the postcodes?

Copy the sentence.

Speech marks need space in a sentence.

Correct the speech marks and capital letters in these sentences. Then copy the sentences.

Where's my other shoe? asked syra.

Don't ask me, replied james, probably in the

shoe cupboard.

Copy the sentence.

Speech marks go around other punctuation.

Correct the speech marks and capital letters in these sentences. Then copy the sentences into your book.

We should go now, jay's dad said, before it

gets dark.

Just a minute, replied amrit. I thought I saw

a badger.

Have you left space for your speech marks?

Time yourself as you quickly copy the passage into your book. Then write in how long it took you to copy it.

Time is the horse that never stops.

It gallops on and on.

Make sure you hold on tight.

The ride is very long.

I can write 23 readable words in _____

_____.

Time yourself as you copy the passage quickly into your book. Write in the time that it takes you to finish.

There are 60 seconds in a minute. There are

60 minutes in an hour.

There are 24 hours in a day. There are 365 and

a quarter days in a year.

There are 10 years in a decade.

There are 100 years in a century.

I can write 45 readable words in _____

_____.

Is your speed writing legible (easy to read)?

29

Copy the words.

recently

bought

replacement

split

Copy the passage neatly, using your best handwriting.

I recently bought a football made by you. After two days of normal play, the ball split. I would like a replacement, please.

Copy the words neatly.

careful

precise

thorough

tidy

Use these words to help you write a polite complaint in your book, using your best handwriting.

- ordered

- delivery

- waiting

- disappointing

Is your writing neat all the way through your letter?

Copy the sentence.

Each item in a list can be several words long.

Add the commas to this list, then copy the sentence.

Beth took a swimming costume a really big towel a set of swimming goggles and a locker token to the swimming pool.

Copy the sentence, changing it into a bullet-pointed list.

We went shopping for our new dog and bought: puppy food, squeaky toys, a soft bed.

-
-
-

Have you left space after your bullet points?

Correct and neatly copy the passage into your book.

I cant do it moaned hamid. Its simply impossible. You shouldnt be so hard on yourself said benji kindly.

How well do you think you have done in your writing?

My tall letters and capitals are the correct height.

My direct speech is in speech marks.

My apostrophes are clearly spaced.

Correct and quickly copy the passage into your book. Time yourself copying it.

Ill never be able to tie my shoelaces Leah protested.

You can do anything you put your mind to and dont forget it said Jared.

I can write 25 readable words in _____

_____.